TRAVEL LIKE A LOCAL-DENVER

Denver Colorado Travel Guide

Taylor Norberg

The statements in this book are of the authors and may not be the views of CZYK Publishing or Greater Than a Tourist.
First Edition
Cover designed by: Ivana Stamenkovic
Cover Image: https://pixabay.com/photos/denver-colorado-city-urban-2230512/

Image 1: By Jeffrey Beall - Own work, CC BY-SA 3.0,
https://commons.wikimedia.org/w/index.php?curid=7455794
Image 2: By Hogs555 - Own work, CC BY-SA 3.0,
https://commons.wikimedia.org/w/index.php?curid=18291324
Image 3: By Sheila Sund -
https://www.flickr.com/photos/sheila_sund/8903465080/in/photolist-eyLzYC-7weu65-
4zc9rT-e8qPxM-akQZbD-7uoUsX-aKvKBx-745E5d-xwHjbZ-7wets3-qiVtjG-5aa1p5-
7XN3Ho-7waFCa-dHsohH-xSioQg-7yg9NK-Q248SP-EWXYaH-4HyfJV-qwqYBe-
fB8TmL-7xb9GG-qQ5XFx-G63EsU-vZbhW5-bAn7KZ-4VDGfU-5fc11k-yL2n7F-
6UwQY2-6nh2i4-qrVEDo-q6U8cD-aBW71j-zTg2ve-9fxoTK-anj3Sv-7BZHSj-ahSaQ2-
aKQ87x-MtyQK1-xmVtDg-anj4st-98CyRD-7Ttaaa-7Twq63-7Tta9t-3NTCME-9De9PT,
CC BY 2.0, https://commons.wikimedia.org/w/index.php?curid=55645369
Image 4: By R0uge - Own work, CC BY-SA 4.0,
https://commons.wikimedia.org/w/index.php?curid=47831553

CZYK Publishing Since 2011.
CZYKPublishing.com
Greater Than a Tourist

Mill Hall, PA
All rights reserved.
ISBN: 9798860528826

BOOK DESCRIPTION

"Travel Like a Local Denver " by Taylor Norberg is your insider's guide to experiencing Denver beyond the usual tourist attractions. Taylor, a Denverite, shares their personal insights and local knowledge to help you uncover hidden gems and authentic experiences in this dynamic city. From RiNo's art scene to LoDo's historic charm and City Park's beauty, explore Denver's unique neighborhoods and savor its cuisine at local eateries and breweries. This book also delves into Denver's history and culture, offering a deeper understanding of the city. Whether you're into outdoor adventures, art, or food, Taylor's recommendations ensure a memorable Denver visit. Discover Denver's heart and soul with this immersive travel companion.

OUR STORY

Traveling is a passion of Travel Like a Local book series creator. Lisa studied abroad in college, and for their honeymoon Lisa and her husband toured Europe. During her travels to Malta, an older man tried to give her some advice based on his own experience living on the island since he was a young boy. She was not sure if she should talk to the stranger but was interested in his advice. When traveling to some places she was wary to talk to locals because she was afraid that they weren't being genuine. Through her travels, Lisa learned how much locals had to share with tourists. Lisa created the Travel Like a Local book series to help connect people with locals. A topic that locals are very passionate about sharing.

TABLE OF CONTENTS

THE GREAT OUTDOORS

WAYS TO BE ACTIVE

SHOPPING

DEDICATION

All my words are dedicated to my Denver companion since day one: Katy Long. We met as interns; we became neighbors turned roommates; now we're sisters. I can't think of Denver without thinking of our countless outdoor adventures, apartment shenanigans, and adulthood obstacles we've overcome together. Just like my own life, Denver is a beautiful place because you're in it.

ABOUT THE AUTHOR

Denver was still flying under the radar as a hot destination to move to when someone briefly suggested it as an option for Taylor's next endeavors. As she was researching post-graduation opportunities, she slowly narrowed her search to Colorado-based companies, then it became just Denver. She had never been to Denver though, so when she traveled there for her interview, it was her first time ever in the Mile High City! Even before arriving, her affinity for Denver had started to grow, so by the time she was offered an internship — although it was only a 3-month gig — she signed a year-long lease (and many more following that). From Florida, she drove her deteriorating sedan 1,700 miles to her new home; meanwhile, her two cats and family hopped on a quick 4-hour flight to meet her there.

Two addresses, four jobs, and many snowboard seasons later, Taylor is a true Denverite. She feels deeply connected to the community, so she dedicates time in a leadership role for a volunteer committee that focuses on barriers to housing stability in Denver. Taylor spends her summers being overly competitive in pick-up volleyball games at the park and her winters slipping on ice patches outside her apartment complex. She adores her city so much that it's only fair she shares her authentic experiences with others looking to explore Denver like a local.

HOW TO USE THIS BOOK

Welcome to the Travel Like a Local Guidebook series! Our mission is to give readers an inside look at travel destinations around the world through the eyes of locals. Each guidebook in this series is written by a local who has explored and experienced the destination in depth. The author has made suggestions based on their own experiences. Please check before traveling to the area in case the suggested places are unavailable.

Travel Advisories: As a first step in planning any trip abroad, check the Travel Advisories for your intended destination.
https://travel.state.gov/content/travel/en/traveladvisories/traveladvisories.html

FROM THE PUBLISHER

Traveling can be one of the most important parts of a person's life. The anticipation and memories that you have are some of the best. As a publisher of the Travel Like a Local, Greater Than a Tourist, East Like a Local, as well as the popular *50 Things to Know* book series, we strive to help you learn about new places, spark your imagination, and inspire you. Wherever you are and whatever you do I wish you safe, fun, and inspiring travel.

Lisa Rusczyk Ed. D.
CZYK Publishing

TRAVEL LIKE A LOCAL

Washington Park

Genesee Park is the largest of the Denver Mountain Parks.

Denver and nearby mountains as seen from the rooftops of the Cherry Creek neighborhood

View of downtown Denver after a snowstorm in March 2016, looking northwest from Cheesman Park

Traveling is like reading a book, the farther you get the more you've learned.

- Unknown

Denver
Colorado, USA

Denver Colorado Climate

	High	Low
January	49	20
February	49	21
March	58	29
April	65	35
May	73	45
June	86	55
July	92	61
August	90	59
September	82	50
October	68	37
November	57	27
December	47	19

GreaterThanaTourist.com

Temperatures are in Fahrenheit degrees.
Source: NOAA

LOCAL TIDBITS

1. DENVER CULTURE 101

As a traveler or potential resident, understanding our city's culture will go a long way during your endeavors. Denver is known to have a social, outdoorsy, and laid-back way of life. A few Denverite stereotypes include owning a dog, driving a Subaru and exclusively supporting locally brewed beer. Friendships blossom quickly in Denver, as everyone seems open to new relationships. There are group meet-ups for every hobby from juggling to crocheting to acro yoga, so you never know when you'll be introduced to your next bestie! The city population has been multiplying from the influx of transplants who are drawn to the mountain range that begins only 45 minutes west of Denver. For some adventure-seekers, Denver is a launching pad to bigger outdoor playgrounds, and for others, it provides ample outdoor activities within city limits. For the city-dwellers who have alternative hobbies, there is a vibrant music and art scene to explore. Denver breeds tons of emerging artists, musicians, chefs, and other talented souls who showcase their work around the city. We're also a hub for start-ups and tech firms, and most of these tenacious companies boast the incredible work-life balance they can offer. For example, during the week, you'll notice our coffee shops filled to the brink with remote workers leisurely sipping iced lattes while on a video meeting. Because of the relatively relaxed work culture here, our downtown is tame compared to a typical businesspeople hustle-bustle.

It's important to note that at this point in the city's history, there's a subtle divide between natives (those who were born and raised here) and transplants. This can cause some contention on ballots or city-ordained policies. As the rush of transplants continues to pour in, the city has been challenged with keeping the transportation and housing demand under control. Despite some growing pains, Denver has a zealous, positive energy that pulses through its people. Every day when I look around my city, I'm incredibly thankful to be a part of this culture.

2. FOUR SEASONS, ONE DAY

Denver is known for having the incredible variety of all four seasons...in one day! A Denverite knows not to check the weather before each day but *throughout* each day. A sunny summer afternoon can turn into a raging hailstorm by nightfall. Or a frigid winter morning can warm up to t-shirt weather by noon. The Denver climate is incredibly sporadic because while we technically sit in a high desert, we get a lot of weather systems that roll over the mountains or come from the north. The good news is that if you have a view of the front range (which many spots in Denver do) then you can see the storms as they approach.

I've learned to keep my wardrobe totally flexible as any one day may require several outfit changes. I've bought a staple jean jacket for tooling around the city, especially during the transitional seasons, fall and spring, as the climate can be extra volatile then. Being open to any possibility is the best mindset to have when planning outdoor activities here. Sometimes we're gifted with a beautiful day on the Platte River, but other days I'll have to retreat indoors when powerful gusts of wind threaten to knock me over. So, when traveling to Denver, don't get stingy on the packing! During most times of the year, it'll be in your favor to include a tank top, boots or closed-toed shoes, long layers, and a light jacket; bathing suits are usually not necessary unless you know you'll be doing a water activity or soaking in a hot tub.

Denver brags about having nearly 300 days of sunshine, so even when it's early February, you'll need to layer on the sunscreen as the UV rays are extremely powerful at this elevation. You may notice your skin and hair getting dehydrated because of our dry climate, so don't forget the lotion, ChapStick, and conditioner on your trip.

A lot of out-of-towners also experience altitude sickness, which is caused by decreased levels of oxygen in the body from being at higher altitudes. This can make visitors experience nausea, dizziness, and headaches. I've seen lots of people get these symptoms from simply walking around Denver, but they will be amplified by going on a strenuous hike or drinking alcohol, so monitor your wellness when you engage in these activities. The good news is that every convenience store is stocked with canisters of oxygen that you can consume to help you feel better. Living in Denver gives me the perspective that I am much smaller than the great natural world around me. By visiting Denver, you will appreciate our mighty Mother Nature in all her moods.

3. HOW TO MAKE I-70 A BREEZE

The main artery of Colorado, I-70, runs east-west coming from Kansas City, directly passing over Denver, then cruising through the Rocky Mountains into Utah. As you can imagine, this route is very well-traveled in both directions by sedans, vans, and semi-trucks alike. Locals frequently use the Colorado Department of Transportation (CDOT)'s Twitter and website page to check for traffic, construction, or accident updates. The absolute busiest time to get on I-70 is a weekend ski day, especially early morning hours and right after the lifts close for the afternoon. As locals, we know to wait out the crowd by staying in the ski lodge until dusk before hitting the road back to Denver. Practicing patience will suit you well when you approach The Eisenhower Tunnel, which requires cars to merge into just two lanes and come to a complete stop before entering.

This is one of the most challenging interstates I've driven on, so I urge you to drive cautiously and read all traffic signs as the roads are often windy with steep grades. I would encourage you to stay in the right lane unless you must pass another vehicle and always stay within the speed limit. It's also important to reference CDOT's resources for any requirement such as winter tires or chains during our winter months. I advise checking the CDOT website or Google Maps before embarking on I-70 at *any* time. Even a seemingly innocent weekday can turn into hours of standstill traffic if one lane is blocked off!

4. AEROTROPOLIS TRAVEL

Located in the flat plains northeast of Denver, lies Aerotropolis. Guarded by "Blucifer", the larger-than-life sculpture of a demonic blue mustang that quite literally killed its creator, is our behemoth of an airport. Denver International Airport (DEN) is currently one of the largest in the nation, acting as an intersection for air travelers coming from all directions. It's riddled with odd artwork such as alien-like portraits that have been the center of conspiracy theories since the inception of the airport. Rumors about the real purpose of our airport range from government hideaways to extraterrestrial housing.

There are mixed reviews from locals about the infrastructure of the airport. Some say it's a breeze to fly through the coveted combo of our Clear and TSA Pre security checkpoints, while others find the enormity of the airport difficult to navigate. The airport has been set up with conveniences such as the RTD Train that runs in frequent intervals to and from Denver's downtown Union Station, as well as a multitude of long-term parking options. When traveling through DEN, I would advise playing it safe by getting to security, which can sometimes wrap around the baggage claim area, two hours before your flight boards. In the event that you have time to spare, DEN has a spectrum of casual to fancy dining options as well as airport-wide WiFi to help you pass the time!

5. WHO RUNS THE TOWN? DOGS.

In our city, the most spoiled residents are our four-legged companions. If you're bringing your pup to Denver, you will have no problem finding them a shady spot at a brewery or an open field for your game of fetch. Dogs seem to be allowed pretty much anywhere here, such as most offices (mine usually has at least three at a time), restaurant patios, and community events. Because of the sheer volume of dogs bopping around town, there is some unspoken etiquette to be followed. For example, if a dog is not friendly amongst other pets it's that owner's responsibility to cross the street or stand far to the side when other animals are approaching. If you're permitting your dog to roam free it's likely going to mingle around, so ensure that the people it socializes with are happy to have a dog in their space.

While there's an abundance of designated off-leash areas, these can get pretty dusty with dirt getting stirred up as pups wrestle around. Instead, my friends go to the off-leash dog meet-up every day at 5 p.m. at Cheeseman Park, which seems to be exempt from park rangers! So far, none of them have ever received a ticket for this technical violation of having their dogs off-leash.

Since we have all four seasons, it's important to prepare your dog for temperatures of both extremes. Owners usually dress their dogs in snow booties and a jacket during the winter months; in summer every dog gets their annual haircut and goes to splash around the Platte River. The occasional outdoor cat (like my two tabbies) is used to scurrying around the neighborhood, so it's crucial that your dog knows its boundaries with our smaller furry friends. Because of all the luxuries for them in Denver, the dogs here are truly living their best lives.

6. GETTING 'ROUND TOWN

Denver is relatively small for a city, so navigating from one side of town to another is usually stress-free! All modes of transportation are available, but I'll give you the rundown of how to use each one to its fullest potential. The Light Rail and bus system (Denver RTD) is still a bit limited for intercity travel because most of the lines have been created for suburban commuters or long-distance excursions. For example, the Light Rail only offers a few stops within the Denver metro before it takes off to the surrounding 'burbs. Locals typically only use the Light Rail for its convenient route from Union Station to the airport or to get to Empower Stadium. Around the downtown area, especially during events such as Rockies games, pedicabs are whizzing by ready to shuttle you to your next destination.

There are not as many bike lanes as I would like to see around the city, but that doesn't stop people from biking or scooting almost everywhere. Most bikers stay off the busiest boulevards like Broadway or Park Avenue, but all the side roads are fair game! There's also a heavily trafficked pedestrian route, called the Cherry Creek Trail, that wraps along the western perimeter of the city, so you can get from one end of Denver to the other in under 30 minutes by bike or scooter. To rent a bike you can stop by Evo, and I would recommend snagging an e-bike to help with any inclines you might face. Wheel Fun is a bike rental shop located in several of our parks, but I'll warn you: they only have cruiser bikes. My parents recently learned these were not ideal for the occasional uphill terrain around Denver.

I would argue that we are more of a Lyft city, so before arriving I would advise you to download the app and get your payment information all squared away. Lyft has taken hold of the electric bike, scooter, and rideshare supply here, so you'll definitely be needing their services at some point! If you've never heard of Turo, I'm here to represent this new car rental app that I'm proudly a part of. Turo allows you to rent locals' cars in the same way you would book an Airbnb. I've had so many out-of-towners rent my car for day trips to the mountains or longer weekend getaways. With so many Turo hosts in Denver, there's no doubt you'll find a car within your price range that's right around the corner so you can easily pick it up and return it without a hassle. Using Turo helps support locals and provides you unmatched convenience!

FOOD & DRINK

7. THE NATIVE PALATTE

While the city represents cuisines from all around the world, there is a specific focus on hearty meat-inspired dishes and southwestern favorites with a Colorado flare. Notice I said meat-*inspired*, meaning a lot of restaurants here cater to vegans as well by putting a cauliflower twist on classics like the cheeseburger (invented in Denver, FYI). The city has done a great job with inclusive food options, so whether you're vegan, gluten-free, or follow a different dietary restriction, you're in good hands here! In this neck of the woods, we serve up lots of gamey mammals like lamb, bison, and venison — only in Denver have I been offered bison tartare!

If you're opting for seafood, make sure you choose a quality establishment as anything they serve you will have been shipped in from the coast. We do have river trout in Colorado, but those fellows are usually too small and lean to provide any real sustenance, so you won't see them on the menus here. Rocky Mountain oysters are considered a delicacy for us, but this infamous dish isn't what you think. When you bite into this crispy, protein-packed appetizer, you're actually eating a bull testicle!

Our interesting climate makes for a very green assortment of produce, so get ready to chow down on lots of asparagus, rhubarb, broccoli raab, zucchini, and parsley. The one fruit we're known for is our Palisade peaches, which come from a western town that has perfect conditions for these peaches to thrive during early summer. There are countless southwestern-style eateries, but many people have noticed we have put our own Denver spin on this cuisine. For example, our unique Colorado green chile is made with pork, tomatoes, and other add-ins to make a thick, spicy sauce. With an interesting blend of livestock, health-conscious options, and mismatched produce, the Colorado cuisine is nothing short of fascinating for any visitor to explore.

8. SO MANY EATERIES AT THE SOURCE

My all-time favorite Denver restaurant lies within the heart of The Source. Before I reveal this five-star gem to you, it's important to know that if you roll up to The Source and don't find my suggestion very compelling, you can pick from a variety of other top-notch options. Sitting in the RiNo neighborhood, The Source is a hotel inspired by Scandinavian and Japanese design elements *and* a culinary complex with exquisite menus. The Source gives a futuristic, airy feel with sleek, colorful accents against a wide-open industrial backdrop.

Within its peripherals, you can dine at Smōk for elevated BBQ, Temaki Den for no-frills sushi, or Grabowski's for Chicago-style pizza. At the top of The Source, you can eat and mingle at The Woods, which is a rooftop bar and restaurant featuring some of the most creative bar food I've ever tried. The Woods is also known for their unobstructed views of downtown meeting the ridges of the front range mountains.

Now for The Source's most impressive culinary contribution: Safta. They serve unmatched Israeli flavors with subtle influences from the Middle East, Europe, and North Africa. Their bone-in lamb shank that cuts like butter is the reason I celebrate every birthday or special occasion at Safta. The restaurant serves family-style, so you'll order plates for the whole table to share. I'm under the impression that everything the chef touches turns to gold, which is why I suggest Safta to every visitor looking for the best meal in Denver.

9. IS BONANNOCONCEPTS TAKING OVER?

Currently taking the Denver food scene by storm is BonannoConcepts. Nine concepts (give or take because they are constantly evolving their portfolio) have been curated from the minds of Frank, Chef, and Jacqueline, Creative Director, Bonanno. The couple has established Italian, French, American, and Mediterranean eateries from the culinary mastermind of Frank Bonanno who is known to frequently visit their establishments and spend time with the crew. According to their website, the chefs at each concept are encouraged to participate in creative exploration of their menus. They say these restaurants breed forward-thinking leaders in the cooking community. Of the current concepts, I dine most regularly at

Osteria Marco located in our lively Larimer Square. This dim-lit Italian tavern serves up decadent pizza and pasta paired with an extensive wine list. No Michelin star has made its mark on Denver yet, but the Bonannos are eager to be the first to receive its coveted status.

At the pinnacle of all their concepts is the Denver Milk Market located in the heart of downtown's Dairy Block, a short walk from Union Station and Coors Field. If you don't know what cuisine you're in the mood for or if you're in a larger group of different preferences, you'll find refuge at Denver Milk Market. A giant donut-shaped bar sits in the center of over a dozen food concepts ranging from poke bowls to ice cream. This elaborate intersection of food and drinks gets especially rowdy during Rockies games or their Sunday Drag Bingo Brunch, which you'll likely see me at! I can't think of a better Friday afternoon than heading downtown to Denver Milk Market for Ahi tacos, a spicy mango marg, and endless possibilities of the night ahead. Rumor has it, they might be switching ownership groups, but the inclusive vibes will stay the same.

10. WE LOVE OUR BREAKFAST & BRUNCH

For those who stay in the city on the weekend, brunch is a sport. Especially when the weather is looking a little fickle, brunch is always a great alternative weekend activity. It's a competitive affair to even book a brunch reservation in Denver, as every single option is incredibly delicious and sought out for. If you're not an early bird, have someone else call ahead or you'll likely be sitting in a lobby for an hour before your name is called!

My absolute favorite brunch spot, located in the Capitol Hill neighborhood, is Jelly. This upgraded, colorful diner serves many elaborate brunch options, but their signature is their mini donut holes that melt in your mouth. Jelly is a known gem, so if you have time to kill time while you're waiting for your table you can grab a coffee at Hudson Hill or check out the iconic record selection at Wax Tracks, both of which are just steps away. If you're a bacon connoisseur, Syrup or Bacon Social should be your go-to! Each offers a variety of bacon plates that range from sweet to savory (personally, anything with brown sugar has my name on it). For a hearty, homestyle meal the locals go to Denver Biscuit Company or Fox Run

Café. At these spots, you'll choose from a menu of classic eggs, meat, and potatoes that'll keep you full for most of the day! My number one vegan brunch place is City'O'City where their meatless chicken and waffles are known across the city. The most popular brunch destination is Snooze A.M. With a whooping four locations in our metro, it's taken reign on Denver's brunch scene. I usually pass up on Snooze A.M. though because wait times can be dizzying, and the experience is less authentic.

With its southwestern influences, Denver is bountiful when it comes to breakfast burrito options as they are an absolute staple in any Denverite's diet. The conversation of the 'best breakfast burrito in town' is always circulating amongst the locals. Santiago's is an ultra-quick, ultra-cheap joint that hits the spot when you need to grab burritos for a large group or when you're in a rush. Bonfire Burritos, originally just a local food truck, are now featured at every coffee shop or Farmer's Market I encounter; these ones are large and packed with protein. Almost all breakfast burritos will come with the option for a side of or smothered-on green chile. Consider this the challenge of your trip: find your opinion of the best breakfast burrito in Denver!

11. FEDERAL BLVD HAS THE HOLE IN THE WALLS

To find the most unpretentious, authentic food in the city, you'll want to pick a spot on S Federal Boulevard. You won't hear about this part of town in the guidebooks because the busy road isn't particularly walkable, so I would suggest having a destination in mind before you set out for your meal. Between 6th Avenue to W Florida Avenue, the street is lined with family-owned restaurants and marketplaces that predominantly serve Hispanic and Asian cuisines. You'll cruise down S Federal Blvd for boba tea, a bowl of pho then finish off with banh mi all from mom-and-pop establishments. When you're in the mood for a flavorful heaping of Pad Thai, my recommendation is Suvipa, but know your heat tolerance before you order your food spicy! The Far East Center and Little Saigon Market (right next to one another) are shopping plazas that transport you to the Eastern world to browse imported products, traditional ingredients, and hand-crafted gifts. Amongst the endless options of tacos, none of which you would go wrong with, the locals recommend Tacos El Pueblita for their quick-serve, inexpensive street tacos. S Federal Boulevard isn't much of a sight-seeing neighborhood, but you'll take a trip there to explore cultural eateries that have been serving locals for generations.

12. SUSHI IS TOTALLY FRESH HERE

Contrary to popular belief (even my own) Denver is oddly prominent in the sushi space. Because Denver is the first inland stop for coastal shipments, we get the freshest fish of any landlocked state. To prove my point, Uchi is a fine-dining sushi experience with an authentically designed interior that holds the title of the best sushi in Denver amongst locals. If you're craving Uchi, but haven't been saving up for it, the locals advise popping in during happy hour (daily, 4-6 p.m.) for a great deal on an otherwise pricey dinner. Sushi Den is a favorite spot for high-quality takeout sushi made with seafood that is flown in daily. At Sushi Den, you can also book the Chef's Table where you'll be seated in front of the sushi as it's being prepared and handpicked by the chef. For a casual sushi experience, I would recommend Izu Sushi on Colfax Avenue. This tiny joint has the best sushi, sashimi, and noodle bowls at reasonable prices.

13. OUR COFFEE SHOPS HIT THE SPOT

Whether you need some pep in your step or just a place to work amongst other people, the coffee shops in Denver will have you covered. For those who love the co-working space environment, Improper City has capitalized on this concept. Techies, entrepreneurs, and remote workers flock to their giant space in RiNo to sip cold brew and connect to the strong WiFi. The vibe at Improper City is social and collaborative, I've even networked with other young professionals there! For a stylish setting, I'd recommend Hudson Hill, which is a chic coffee and cocktail bar that also serves dainty pastries. Pablo's on Sixth is a dive-y coffee shop with board games and funky décor. The last time I checked they did not have WiFi, which makes Pablo's ideal for catching up with friends. I also must give a nod to my woman-owned neighborhood coffee shop Cooper Door, which sits at the edge of the Denver Botanical Gardens and Cheeseman Park. Its location makes it the perfect place to stop in for an iced coffee while on your stroll through our delightful part of town. For a true hidden gem, I encourage you to visit Weathervane. This historic house was converted into a charming coffee shop lined with art and thriving foliage. They have unique sandwich options and unparalleled coffee flavors such as Rose or Smoky Maple.

14. EMBARK ON THE DENVER BEER TRAIL

Just like any other western mountain city, we do not fall short when it comes to breweries. The most famous brand to originate out of Colorado is Coors, whose brewery can be visited in the neighboring town of Golden, but the real charm is found in our local spots. We have over 100 taprooms throughout the Denver metro ranging from open-concept industrialized buildings to microbreweries tucked in alleyways. To visit the most amount breweries in one go, you'll need to head to the RiNo neighborhood where there's a brewery every block! A lot of local beer companies have made it beyond just their four walls; for example, in all our stores, you'll see the colorful, artistic cans of Great Divide that come in all sorts of IPA, lagers, ales, and stouts. Great Divide Brewing Co is a classic amongst locals, so you can never go wrong when showing up with a case of their beer in hand. The Blue Moon's location in the RiNo neighborhood is a sleek open-air building that showcases its process behind floor-to-ceiling windows. I love that they offer experimental flavors only available at this location – they've come around to my table with samplers that included a brand-new chocolate coffee pour!

Upon taking a poll I found that Cerebral Brewing was the most recommended brewery amongst my peers. Their selection ranges from seltzer to stouts so anyone, regardless of their affinity level for beer, will find a drink they love. This neighborhood hangout strives to give back to the community by engaging in non-profit work around the city.

Wynkoop Brewing Company was established in the 1980s as the first brewpub in town, which kicked off a brewery culture that now runs thick through Denver's veins.

15. CAN YOU KEEP THESE SPEAKEASIES A SECRET?

I'm not *supposed* to be telling you this... but Denver is home to some fascinating speakeasies and here's your golden ticket in. In Cherry Creek, stationed under a hotel, is a dim-lit cocktail bar with bartenders in fancy white button-downs pouring sophisticated martinis. This exclusive "members-only" bar is called Boys & Girls Club Denver. To reach this most secretive speakeasy, you'll map yourself to Cherry Creek's Halcyon Hotel, but instead of entering its main doors go down the alley between 2nd and 3rd Avenue until you reach a sign identifying "Stair 3" with a golden doorbell. A hostess will take you down long corridors into the belly of the hotel until you've reached a nook that's humming with conversation. They have a website with a phone number to text for their required reservations, but that's all I can give you, good luck!

The most famous speakeasy in town is unfortunately no longer a well-kept secret, but still a fun adventure, nonetheless. Williams & Graham is now searchable on Google Maps, but when you arrive, you'll be blocked by a pretty convincing bookstore. You'll tell the host you'd like a reservation and when the time comes a bookshelf will reveal the secret passageway. Be prepared for long wait times by grabbing a drink at Recess, the sprawling bar-slash-beer garden next door.

If you want to skip the classic Prohibition-era ambiance, there's a hidden bar within an ice cream parlor that has a neon red aesthetic instead. The freezer within the Frozen Matter ice cream shop marks the entrance to Retrograde. Once you're let in, you'll be under glowing lights and sipping space-themed cocktails. Can I trust that you will keep these top-secret locations totally confidential?

NEIGHBORHOODS

16. ART DISTRICTS WITH COLORFUL MURALS

Several artistic neighborhoods across the town are home to quirky shops, art galleries, and interesting events. The Santa Fe Arts District is the smallest of these, centered mainly around Santa Fe Drive from about 6th to 13th Street. This main road is enveloped in a cultural hub that is rich in Latino heritage. Exploring the Santa Fe Arts District means popping into any of the diverse creative spaces such as Museo de las Americas or Center for Visual Art and then grabbing a bite at Chuey FU's for unique Latin-Asian grub. In this neighborhood, you can walk the side streets of funky houses then stroll into any of the art galleries or maybe even the antique shop to immerse yourself in a new world.

In our northern part of town is the RiNo Arts District, where you can spend the afternoon sightseeing the immaculate murals and tasting local brews. Known for our love of beer, Denverites commandeer in RiNo for its endless choices of micro and commercial breweries such as Our Mutual Friend and Ten Barrel. For those non-beer lovers, don't fret because the district is also equipped with full-service bars that turn the streets into a party after dark. Locals go to Beacon to wander through their immersive rooms while bopping to house music. Across the street is Larimer Lounge where they serve up cheap drinks and any genre of live music. In this area, you'll start at Los Chingones and begin wandering down Larimer Street. You may want to begin with a coffee at the Denver Central Market or a craft cocktail at Death & Company. Once you've spotted as many murals as possible, come back along Walnut Street for even more boutiques and art shops. In the summer, you'll notice people taking a different mode of transportation: Bike bars, which allow patrons to sip and pedal through the lively streets. RiNo will open your imagination to a world of virtuous conceptions.

17. HISTORY IN CAPITOL HILL

Historic estates, walkable coffee shops, a park on a rolling hill with the mountains' silhouettes on its horizon. This is my all-time favorite neighborhood and the one I currently reside in: Capitol Hill. This charming slice of garden-grunge has absolutely stolen my heart. I can take a walk around the neighborhood and see something new every time. Every single house, whether it's been standing since 1890 or 2010 has its own fascinating character to it. In this part of town, vines grow up brick walls, sunshine splashes into courtyards and dogs live better than humans.

My neighborhood of Capitol Hill starts at the State Capitol Building, which can be an interesting place to take a free tour or attend one of its city-wide events. The Capitol is trying to establish itself more in the community by hosting events such as Denver Pride Fest, big-name concerts, and the Denver Christmas Market. To the east of our Capitol, you'll stumble upon vegan cafes, small concert venues, a refill shop, and plenty of dispensaries along 13th Street. As you continue further, your eyes will be darting every which way to take in the neighborhood's peculiar residents, bushes of bright foliage and marvelous mini-mansions. Don't let the term "mini mansion" be misleading though; this pocket of town has converted most of its ginormous homes into multifamily living. I once resided in a house with a total of 10 tenants (2 per floor — I was in the basement)! With so many people packed into what used to be a residential piece of Denver, we're always out and about. Bikes, scooters, hoover boards, and runners with dogs in tow will be zooming by you.

After a lovely walk, I encourage you to cool off by getting a cone at our corner ice cream shop, Lik's Ice Cream – the line out the door may look intimidating, but it moves remarkably fast! If you need a bite to eat you could grab a juicy sandwich from SubCulture, indulge in a delicious Italian meal at Angelo's, or order a gyro from the walk-up counter at Chef Zobra's. At the center of it, all is Cheeseman Park, a green paradise that backs up to the Denver Botanical Gardens. The Pavilion is an outdoor, marble structure perched at the tallest point of the park where you never know what event might be going down. It's been a place for weddings, prom pictures, roller skating, biker meet-ups, and anything else I could think of. Our park is full of energy as dogs roam freely and groups are scattered on the lawn picnicking, tanning, or playing.

18. DOWNTOWN ALONG THE RIVER

We have two adjacent neighborhoods that offer the urban lifestyle, which are LoDo and Highlands. LoDo (Lower Downtown) is our main business and entertainment district. Start your journey at Union Station which is an indoor/outdoor plaza of restaurants and bars centered around our grand train station that bustles with travelers and commuters. You'll then make your way to Blake Street heading toward Coors Field by walking through our grid of modern and brick buildings. After marveling at our iconic outdoor baseball stadium, take a right up 20th Street to get to Commons Park. Here you'll find a well-occupied skate park and grass fields overlooking the Confluence River rapids.

A pedestrian bridge leads you into the Highlands neighborhood that overlooks the downtown skyline. This area is populated with modern townhomes and the trendiest spots such as Little Man's Ice Cream that always has a line stretching around the block. End your downtown escapade in Larimer Square, a lively block filled with some of the best-rated restaurants in Denver such as Bao Brewhouse, which turns into a dance club after dark (I've once been served free bao buns while just waiting in line).

Downtown offers abundant dining and entertainment possibilities while still keeping a green space at the center of it all.

19. FANCY FOLK GO TO CHERRY CREEK

In the southeast corner of Denver lies our upscale financial district. Cherry Creek does not shy away from its reputation of bougie, high-end living. In this neighborhood, real estate agencies, designer brands, and big banks have set up shop. Since this area is a hub for networking professionals, the busiest parts of the day are during lunch break and happy hour. For a walk through the neighborhood, you'll aptly start at the Whole Foods then mosey down 2nd or 3rd Ave, where you'll treat yourself to some lavish apparel or home goods if your credit card allows.

The Cherry Creek Shopping Center consists of excellent-quality products on the first floor, but just wait, once you head up the escalator, you're walking amongst even more luxurious stores in a much quieter atmosphere. The AMC Movie Theater within the mall is a sparkling clean, comfortable setting to watch the next box office hit while being served at your seat.

For an outdoor experience, you can hit par at the Denver Country Club or swing your racquet at the energetic Gates Tennis Center. The neighborhood is also home to unique fitness experiences such as SoulCycle (high-energy cycling classes) or CLIMBR (strenuous endurance workouts with high-tech machinery). Those looking for an opulent experience will feel right at home strolling the posh shops and candle-lit restaurants under the twinkling string lights of Cherry Creek.

20. THE QUIRKY CHARACTER OF CITY PARK

The largest green space in the Denver metro can be found on the east side of the City Park neighborhood. It contains a community golf course, the Denver Zoo, and a huge pavilion overlooking a pond with a roaring fountain in the center. The park has wide open fields perfect for that game of ultimate frisbee you've always wanted to try or matured trees for groups to find refuge under the shade. Pathways are sprawling throughout the park so you can meander amongst runners and bikers before laying down your picnic blanket.

You'll also notice the park shares its borders with the Denver East Highschool, which seriously looks like a palace and is worth taking a gander at! With so much foot traffic, the park is always buzzing with events such as their weekly Farmer's Market or the Jazz in the Park summer series.

Once you've traversed the trail around City Park, you'll head into the heart of the neighborhood where you'll find quaint cafes wedged within the picturesque estates. For lunch, grab a bite at Dos Santos for high-quality street-style tacos on their rustic outdoor patio. If you're up for a bizarre experience, duck inside The Thin Man bar where you'll be welcomed by cultish emblems under a faint red glow. The residents of this part of town live in old, multilevel homes that are now split into apartments, but despite the modernizations, nothing here has lost its charm.

ARTS, ENTERTAINMENT & EVENTS

21. GET LOST AT THE SANTA FE ART WALK

Standing out amongst the dozens of art walks hosted around the city, is the most captivating one of them all: First Fridays on Santa Fe. On the first Friday of every month (Denverites love their commitment to year-round, rain or shine!) the Santa Fe Arts District blossoms into an atmosphere of festival proportions. Food trucks line the side streets and pedestrians swarm the storefronts, which means this event is most suitable for those who don't mind crowds or cramped spaces. There's no order of operations to follow, so feel free to peruse the shops in any nonlinear fashion you'd like. One minute you'll be gawking at life-size wooden carvings of monstrous creatures, but the next you'll be in a glow-in-the-dark warehouse wondering where that futuristic music is coming from. Because of the masses it draws, parking is impossible, so I suggest arriving via rideshare, scooter, or the RTD Train that has a stop close by.

My advice to you is that no secret passageway or nondescript door is off-limits. I have stumbled into a ritualistic Krav Maga showcase and discovered my favorite local jeweler by getting lost in an unmarked gallery. My partner once bought a historic map of his random hometown suburb because we ended up in an attic full of antique paintings. Every shop's doors are flung wide open, welcoming all who dare to enter. Our First Friday Art Walk is a space to ask questions, partake in a new experience and go far beyond your comfort zone.

22. CASA BONITA: BACK AND BETTER THAN EVER

At the pinnacle of absurdity, you'll find a pink palace with a perplexing entertainment concept and an even more outrageous backstory. Locals know that Casa Bonita, just west of Denver, originated in the '70s as a restaurant-slash-performing arts extravaganza serving abysmal Mexican food topped with neon orange cheese that routinely turned patrons' stomachs over. However, the lure of table-side mariachi bands and a full-blown cliff-diving show kept people coming back just for the comedic insanity of it all. High schoolers were hired to throw tricks off the waterfall's platform while a gorilla mascot ran loose. The original version of the restaurant was clearly surviving off its one-of-a-kind atmosphere that hosted a mystical cave and jungle-like diving hole.

In recent years though, Casa Bonita seemed to be on its final chapter and had even filed for bankruptcy, until some unlikely heroes stepped in to keep the legacy alive. Locals should've known that when Casa Bonita was the *only* real business ever featured in Comedy Central's South Park series, they could count on the creators to save the day. From the minds of South Park, Trey Parker and Matt Stone are now onto their next project of revitalizing Casa Bonita by preserving all the charisma but elevating the food. With a $40 million renovation budget, the new owners aimed to polish up (and enhance the safety of) the existing facilities while also adding four bars and a prominent executive chef to right the previous kitchen's wrongs. The new, refined menu only offers eight signature entrees to choose from. Don't worry about still feeling hungry though, with your ticket you'll also receive chips and salsa, and they're self-proclaimed famous sopapillas. Casa Bonita is a beloved Denver attraction that will never let its flame die out.

23. MEOW WOLF ISN'T WHAT IT SEEMS

Step inside an intergalactic transportation post to crack the curious case of the missing travelers or simply observe the sweeping art depictions of the multiverse. Convergence Station, the third Meow Wolf location, is a mysterious narrative, a colossal art exhibit, and a cosmic-inspired event space. I wouldn't judge if you visited this tourist destination *twice* because of how expansive the story and rooms are. If you've only got one visit to take it all in, opt for a second walk around the museum because you'll find plenty of new sights the next time you lap it. A visit takes no less than two hours to even scratch the surface, and I guarantee you'll leave with more questions than answers.

The mystery, which is totally optional and completely unsolvable (but fascinating), is about several lifeforms who disappear during a sci-fi event that has warped the space-time continuum. To follow along you'll purchase a memory card at the front entrance where you'll unlock pieces of the puzzle at glowing stations placed throughout the rooms. I've tried my hand at this mystery, but the clues are so elaborate I'm convinced I only found a fragment of them. To explain the outrageous level of detail, there's a library-themed room that has *handwritten* diaries from the characters spanning hundreds of pages each.

The second time I visited Meow Wolf, I went purely for the artistic lure. Each room is designed by a unique individual who is interrupting the story in their own abstract way. You might come across a crawl space with a crooked path that flips you sideways or a junkyard of self-playing instruments conducting eerie sounds that never really materialize into music. The best rooms have hidden entrances so make sure you check behind every door and go down all the stairwells. When you reach one of the main rooms that has a conglomerate of towering neon pillars, you'll see people fiddling with a system of levers in the upper left corner. Visitors hardly get these levers to do their job, so sneakily pull a staff member aside (they're dressed as aliens) and ask them to "Open the sky". If they oblige, you'll get to see an incredible light show on the ceiling – everyone will thank you.

24. DENVER AFTER DARK

When the sun settles below the front range, several major streets turn congested with boisterous partygoers, greasy food trucks, and hustling Lyft drivers. Our four biggest clubs populate Broadway from 12th to 10th Avenue where they compete for the loudest music and longest lines. Church is, you guessed it, a restored church now blasting dance beats under preserved stained-glass windows. Temple is a venue where you can attend an EDM concert in their Vegas-like atmosphere. Club Vinyl is a multi-level space that changes music genres from electronic to hip-hop as you ascend the different floors. In my opinion, Milk Bar is the most entertaining of all the clubs on Broadway because of its endless labyrinth of eccentric rooms. On your adventure through the hazy, sticky chambers, you might wind up in the disco era, the emo-punk age, or in the nostalgia of a 70s arcade. When traversing through Milk Bar, make sure to keep your friends close, because one wrong turn could get you separated for the whole night; you can even designate a meet-up area such as the Red Room where you can reunite to the tune of remixed hits.

In downtown, you'll find a standard bar scene that plays the typical Top 40s, so to escape the basic, I suggest ducking into Herb's for a crowded dance floor that's belting classics performed by a live band. If you're downtown wanting an offbeat vibe, you can meander over to Honor Farm where a giant skeleton looms over you while you sip a truly unusual craft cocktail. In the attic of this artistic bar, you'll see a lifeguard manning the entrance to a hideaway called Hell or Highwater, which has such authentic beach shack décor that you'll think you've landed in a fisherman's fantasy.

Our RiNo district is the other main destination for nighttime shenanigans. The neighborhood has a long stretch of Larimer Street with pedestrian-only blocks where you can safely hop from Meadowlark, the forest-y bar with a tree growing in the middle of its patio, to Finn's Manor, the casual outdoor spot for delicious drinks. Once you've decided on your vibe for the night, you won't be disappointed with what Denver nightlife has to offer.

25. YOU MAY HAVE HEARD OF RED ROCKS

Just a twenty-minute drive outside of Denver lies our natural amphitheater that draws in crowds and acts from all over the globe. Red Rocks Amphitheatre is marked by two monumental rock formations on either side of the stage that immerse you in a world of your own. The biggest names in music and entertainment stop here on the weekends during spring-fall months and you can catch lesser-known acts on the weekdays.

As your Denver guide, I can't stress this enough: Be prepared for crazy weather at this outdoor theater. I've seen cars destroyed by hail, people slipping on the flooded stairs and friends shivering when the sun goes down. I would advise checking the weather immediately before heading over to the show and always airing on the side of caution with warmer layers and rain gear. Several shows take place during winter where the audience is encouraged to wear literal ski suits!

To see its glory in a less crowded form, Red Rocks is usually open to the public for recreation during non-show times. Fitness enthusiasts do workouts in the stands while others just take in the views and hop on stage to envision the perspective of a rockstar. There are also easy trails surrounding Red Rocks, so you can hike through the foothills with our iconic venue as the backdrop. Red Rocks also hosts non-musical events such as morning yoga classes or movie nights for families.

Taking Ubers and Lyfts is totally commonplace for getting here, but cell service gets pretty limited when you're exiting the grounds with thousands of other people, so scheduling a pickup time is always advised. Big groups will opt for party buses that they pre-book for drop off and pick up; this can also be economically friendly if you have a group of over 15. There are also shuttle services, such as Bus To Show, that leave Denver from a designated location and drop you back off afterward. These communal buses can be super unruly, so be prepared to embrace the blaring music and screaming concertgoers! If your crew has a designated driver, another great option is to drive yourselves and tailgate. There's plenty of parking if you get to the show before doors open, which gives you the perfect excuse to prop up the lawn chairs and pregame in the lot. You may also be in for a stellar workout when visiting Red Rocks because the farther away you park or get dropped off, the more stairs you'll be climbing. Don't be intimated though, the adrenaline of being at Red Rocks helps you power through even the steepest uphill trek.

26. BUT LET'S GO BEYOND RED ROCKS

Denver's thriving music scene goes far beyond the allure of Red Rocks Amphitheatre, which surprised me when I first arrived. Every major neighborhood has multiple venues, in fact, five concert halls are walkable from my house alone! I would have to say the most popular genres played in Denver are jam bands (think: Phish), modern psychedelic rock (think: Tame Impala), and EDM (think: GRiZ), but don't get me wrong, I've also gone moshing to heavy metal and swaying to reggae here. The jam band influence stems from The Grateful Dead, who are legends to Denverites. Their band symbol (a half-blue, half-red skull with a lightning bolt through the middle) is plastered all over the town on cars, storefronts, and artwork. There are bars named after this band and every older local has a story about going to one of their epic shows. Dead & Company (feat. notable artists like John Mayer) frequently came around to riff for hours, but the reunion group is officially *dead* now. I have a feeling that won't be the last of The Grateful Dead tribute bands though.

The best venue in Denver, in terms of cleanliness, organization, and sound quality is Mission Ballroom. At this newly built venue mid-size to big-name acts play under the massive disco ball and there's never a line for drinks or the bathroom. For a completely opposite experience, I go to Larimer Lounge, which is a dive-y live music bar that plays anything from rock to techno. You likely won't have heard of the musicians that go on stage here, but the dance floor is always electric, and I have a hard time leaving Larimer Lounge at the end of the night. Along Colfax Ave there are several old-school theaters situated close together that present shows every night of the week. These classic concert halls are The Filmore, The Bluebird, and The Ogden where the crowd is packed in tight. For funk, EDM, and pop-up art galleries, I go to Cervantes where the audience likes it groovy, and the main act usually goes on at midnight.

27. FEELIN' FRESH AT THE FARMER'S MARKET

While Denver isn't particularly known for our produce, we still fill our Farmer's Markets with fresh goodies. The produce usually consists of greens and veggies, so think anything from carrots and asparagus to all types of lettuce, while citrus or fruits can be pretty sparing here. I also see my friends snagging freshly made delicacies like hummus, salsas, and green chiles.

The Farmer's Markets in town are as much a social affair as a grocery run. Sometimes you'll come just to meet up with friends for breakfast burritos and cold brew coffees. I've spent plenty of time at Farmer's Markets just lounging on nearby patches of grass solely to chat with neighbors and meet new dogs. The largest, busiest one in Denver is the Pearl Street Farmer's Market, taking place every Sunday morning from May to November – and they emphasize *rain or shine*. The long stretch of stalls can get really crowded by mid-morning, so the locals know to go bright and early when the market opens at 9 a.m. If you're looking for a more laid-back, neighborhood option, I would recommend the City Park Farmer's Market. You'll notice this is a relatively small group of vendors, but it's much more social as people gather on the lawn and around the fountain to enjoy their morning. This is located at City Park Esplanade and spans the same time frame from May through November, except is held on Saturdays, so if you're ambitious you could go to both for a different experience at each!

28. ROOT FOR THE HOME TEAMS

With six professional sports teams, Denver has no shortage of fanatics crawling around the city on gamedays (especially since online gambling is legal here). Each sporting event has a different vibe, so you can choose according to your mood. In the heat of our dry summers, Coors Field is filled with fans in purple baseball jerseys who are there for the large beers and views of the mountains. The crowd at our Rockies games is relatively laid back and locals are known for going to the game, but not actually *watching* it. For the most social experience, you can mingle by the bars on The Rooftop section where you might only catch a glimpse of the diamond every now and then, but the lively atmosphere is what it's all about. For the cheapest seats, people will congregate in the Rock

Pile: our free-for-all outfield bleachers that get brutally hot during day games.

In my opinion, the most electric games happen inside Ball Arena where the three-time Stanley Cup clinchers, the Avalanche, pass the puck and the Nuggets shoot three-pointers. When I need an adrenaline rush, I get tickets to hear the roar of the crowd in the jam-packed indoor arena that's right downtown. Denver is a top contender in both hockey and basketball, which makes for sold-out games all year long at this venue. The Denver Nuggets won their first NBA Championship title in 2023, so I can't even imagine how vivacious the upcoming basketball seasons are going to be! Our city even has a top-tier college hockey team, the Denver University Pioneers, who have won the NCAA Frozen Four title a whopping nine times.

The Broncos, our NFL team, play at Empower Field in the fall so be sure to bring the winter coat because they'll play snow or shine. Their stadium is on the west outskirts of Denver, so it's accessible by our RTD light rail, Uber, and scooter. Unfortunately for me, my favorite sport, soccer, is played at DICK'S Sporting Goods Park near the airport. The Rapids draw fans in with a supporter section that beats the drum to catchy chants. With our variety of sports, there's almost always a game going on no matter the time of year.

29. THE BEST VIEW OF DENVER

I bet a lot of travel blogs mention the 16th Street Mall as a destination worth visiting, but I would advise against it when you're looking for a local experience. This is a long outdoor promenade through downtown that is lined with chain restaurants, gift shops, and fast fashion stores not unique to the Denver area. As of 2023, this stretch of 16th Street has been overtaken by construction projects, which makes accessing the strip very difficult. In the center of 16th Street Mall is the Denver Pavilions, which is a multi-level conglomerate of bars, shops, and a very rundown movie theater that once took me 30 minutes to exit because of a creaky elevator and a maze of stairwells. Somehow Denver Pavilions has capitalized on the keyword search for "best view of Denver", but for obvious reasons, I have two alternatives for you.

The best view of the mountains from downtown Denver can be found at Peaks Lounge. This cocktail bar on the top floor of our Hyatt Regency is set up with floor-to-ceiling west-facing windows so you can see sweeping views of the front range mountains while sipping a handcrafted drink. In contrast, the best view of our city skyline can be found at Avanti Food & Beverage. At sunset, you'll grab a bite from one of their many food stalls then head to their outdoor patio to enjoy the orange sun reflecting off the city's glass buildings.

30. THE LIVE SHOWS DON'T DISAPPOINT

Although we're most known for our musical acts, other forms of great talent are around every corner. For the best drag shows in town, you should visit the Denver Milk Market for their Sunday Drag Bingo Brunch where you might laugh so hard you won't hear the bingo number they call. Across town, Hamburger Mary's hosts their colorful drag extravaganzas in a close-up and interactive setting. Our Comedy Works in downtown brings in well-known stand-ups, while Denver Comedy Underground on Colfax showcases our city's rising talent against a brick backdrop. For a more immersive show, The Dinner Detective Murder Mystery will serve you gala-like entrees of steak while you participate in solving a crime. The biggest productions that come to town are held at the Denver Center for Performing Arts. From Broadway musicals to seasonal shows, this complex is comprised of more than five theaters that showcase a variety of entertainment acts.

For the rough-and-tumble folk, or those willing to see something unconventional, the National Western Complex hosts rodeos, monster trucks, and its famous Stock Show. For a whole month the Stock Show brings in ranchers from far and wide, so don't be alarmed when you witness hundreds of bolo ties and longhorns parading down 17th Street to kick off the annual festivities!

31. TIME FOR SOME FRIENDLY COMPETITION

For group activities or a change of pace from brewery hopping, Denverites love to play games. We have two 1Up's, an arcade bar with sticky floors where locals hang out for cheap drinks, and copious rounds of Skee-Ball. The atmosphere at 1Up is dark, loud, and grungy, so if you're looking for a cleaner experience, I would recommend Lucky Strike, which has a more loungey vibe with a full-service bar and restaurant. Lucky Strike is equipped with a bowling alley and a room of gigantic, neon-lit games such as an entire wall consisting of Pac-Man.

If you like to play billiards, you might stack up pretty well against the competition by heading to Wynkoop Brewery, Zanzibar, or Gerard's for first-come first-serve pool games with other locals. Our most impressive glow-in-the-dark minigolf course is undergoing renovations, but you can still play at Aqua Golf or Puttshack while the other one gets an upgrade. Denver has also adopted axe throwing as a casual bar sport (questionable, I know), which is why we've welcomed Bad Axe Throwing into our mix of entertainment options. If axe throwing doesn't release enough rage for you, try SMASH*IT Breakroom to obliterate old computers with a wrecking tool of your choosing. These spots around town will bring out your competitive spirit for all your friends to witness.

32. WATCH YOUR BACK ON OUR GHOST TOURS

With less than 800,000 *living* souls in Denver, it's no wonder we're quite outnumbered by those in the afterlife. The remains of over 2,000 bodies still toss and turn in their crevices 6 feet below Cheeseman Park's happy-go-lucky grassy surface. This underground world is filled with resentful spirits who were buried in the cemetery, which was the original purpose of the grounds. They were forgotten about as laborers rushed to meet the city's demands of flipping it into a park. To make matters more disturbing, the caskets for the job were so tiny that many corpses had to be dismembered just to get shoved into the cramped boxes. Meanwhile, looters showed no mercy for the dead as they rummaged around to score expensive heirlooms right off the human remains.

The mansions hold just as sinister secrets as the park they surround because this neighborhood was established for the greedy elite who committed harrowing sins to collect their riches. Our city's ghost tours will wind you through streets of haunted manors in Capitol Hill until you descend upon the park all while hearing details of this eerie history. Of the three houses in the Netflix documentary *28 Days Haunted,* a show where paranormal specialists spend a month investigating the supernatural world within each estate, one was right here in Denver.

33. MOLLY BROWN WAS MORE THAN A SURVIVOR

You may recall Kathy Bates' character in James Cameron's rendition of *Titanic* as an elite woman with relatively good intentions compared to her privileged peers. This was an authentic portrayal of Denver homeowner and Titanic survivor Molly Brown. Her rags-to-riches story brought her to the famous house in Denver — where she resided before her global travels led her aboard the Titanic — which has now been transformed into a historic museum. The stone house, accented in orange details, is guarded by lion and pharaoh statues that have all been restored to their original magnificence by Historic Denver, Inc. At this landmark, you'll learn that surviving the Titanic was only a mere sliver of her incredible life participating in philanthropy, advocacy, and adventure.

The museum takes you through when she first found fortune by literally striking gold, all the way to her post-Titanic life of fighting for labor equality and women's suffrage. The museum also holds artifacts from her life such as jewelry, garments, and furniture that will transport you into the world of the wealthy during the Victorian era. You can take a guided tour through the collections or embark on your own self-explorations. The museum also focuses on other pivotal events during this time such as technological takeaways from the 1800s World Fairs. While you'll learn all about the tragedy of the Titanic, the museum aims to bring you the bigger picture of society during that era.

34. A DAM GOOD TIME

It's only fitting that the center of our city holds a museum complex that brings an array of cultures and regions together. Sandwiched between our state capitol, the public library, and several historic centers is a pointy origami-like building. The Denver Art Museum (DAM), despite its incredibly futuristic physique, does not display many modern exhibits. Instead, it will showcase well-known fine art from all corners of the world such as the empowering collection of Freida Kahlo or textiles from ancient Africa.

Because of Colorado's rich Native American history, the DAM was an early adopter of Indigenous artwork compared to other cultural institutions in North America. DAM has made a commitment to not only present historic Indigenous works, but also elevate their contemporary voices every step of the way. The museum invites originality during their drop-in drawing and writing sessions where participants are guided by creative professionals who help inspire the imagination. There are also more formal classes available such as a candle-making workshop of the four-week long course that explores what happens when natural ingredients meet experimental art. The DAM is a welcoming, peaceful environment where education and diverse perspectives are celebrated.

THE GREAT OUTDOORS

35. A LOVELY STROLL THROUGH THE BOTANICAL GARDENS

Tucked behind Cheeseman Park, lies a flourishing oasis of otherworldly plant life. The gardens have created an environment for native and foreign species to coexist peacefully in, so you'll walk by everything from cacti with needles as thick as fingers to a giant bed of neon tulips. To be fair, I'm a huge advocate of the Botanical Gardens as I've lived across the street for years and have even worked on their website for a pro-bono project! I have seen firsthand how pinnacle this green space is to our community. Locals and tourists alike are drawn here for all types of reasons. The gardens are a lovely urban haven for those needing to connect with nature as well as an engaging opportunity for researchers or plant enthusiasts who want to dive deeper. The crowds start with school kids and elders coming to enjoy the serenity in the early mornings then by sunset it becomes a gathering place for young adults to unwind.

The gardens are open for visitation year-round, so even when the blooming season (May-June) is long gone, they'll make sure there's still something special to see. In fact, the dead of winter might somehow be their busiest time as they host Light Up the Gardens where every branch on the premise is wrapped in glimmering holiday lights. There's also an abundance of educational opportunities for children and curious adults such as teachings and interactive programs on subjects spanning from cultural history to plant care. During warmer months, there is always yoga, meditation, happy hours, or concerts to attend. Once you enter the gardens you have endless possibilities of exploration. You can tour the newly built Freyer–Newman Center, which showcases art, film, a library, and a coffee shop selling plants. Then you can transport yourself to a tropical climate in the huge conservatory that keeps itself undeniably humid. The main part of the gardens consists of an outdoor stroll through sections of fascinating plant life that you haven't even fathomed yet! There's no doubt that the Denver Botanical Gardens brings the entire community together for a greater purpose and passion, so I would absolutely urge you to experience the enchantment for yourself.

36. WHERE TO SPLASH AROUND

In this high desert climate, summers can only be survived by finding refuge in water. Scoping out our natural swimming pools has required dedication because nearby water can be murky with city runoff, but the farther you go the more frigid it becomes. The apex where our two rivers converge downtown in front of the REI building is a park for families and dogs to cool off. At this spot, Commons Park, the water's quality varies depending on seasonality and rain frequency, but if it's moving at a good pace then I would say you're in the clear to dive in! Soda Lakes and Horsetooth Reservoir are both in neighboring towns, so people flock to either of these options on sunny days to paddleboard or swim below the foothills.

I'm a huge fan of experiencing our rivers via Innertube, so when I'm looking for a wild ride, I go down the Clear Creek in Golden and for a mellow day I float the South Platte River in Littleton. To tubes our rivers, I would advise renting water shoes so your feet don't go numb in our snowmelt water and so you have stable footing on the rocky riverbed. On the semi-intense whitewater route in Golden, you'll want to wear a helmet because it'd be a miracle if you *don't* flip out at some point. The best advice I've been given was when a teenage raft guide told me the technique is to lean forward down the river – if you lean back, you're just asking for the rapids to swallow you up. When tubing, you can either buy a shuttle pass from the rental shop if available, walk along the river to get back to your starting point, or plant two cars at both ends of your excursion. I would suggest calling rental companies ahead of time to verify that the river is open for use. In recent summers, the flow has been so powerful we've had to wait weeks for water levels to go down! Although Colorado is a landlocked state, the locals know there's just as much adventure in our water as there is on dry land.

37. ADVENTURE AT CHEERY CREEK STATE PARK

The Cherry Creek State Park requires a small fee to enter, but once inside you can wander through acres of preserved meadowland while dozens of prairie dogs pop out of their dwelling holes to greet you. The park has 35 miles of mixed-use trails that wind around the reservoir, through the wooded forest, and across the rolling fields. If you're in need of some puppy love, there's a rambunctious off-leash section where dogs roam free, wrestle one another, and splash in the creek. This section is massive, so make sure to keep your dog within close sight and ensure they're friendly with other pups!

It's a serious juxtaposition when I can hear the rhythmic sounds of waves crashing just outside my landlocked city. When staying in Denver you can channel your love of water at the Cherry Creek Reservoir, which sits inside the Cherry Creek State Park, where you'll be amongst kayaks, paddleboarders, small boats, and sopping wet dogs. The Cherry Creek Reservoir is a manmade lake that can almost pass as an urban beach. There's pebbly sand that you can lay out on, grills for group picnics, or comfortable-temperature water that's available for any activity including swimming. It's a true lake day as I'm basking in the sun on a floatie whilst jet skis whir past. If you didn't happen to bring a motorboat on your travels, you can set up shop on the beachy shorelines or take to the open waters by joining a sailing class. The Cherry Creek State Park has become my refuge when I'm itching for a nearby retreat into nature.

38. A MILE INTO THE WILD

From an elevated walkway, you can peacefully observe extraordinary animals without interfering in their unrestricted environment. A tad north of Denver, The Wild Animal Sanctuary is home to about 750 wild animals who have been liberated from inhumane living conditions and rehabilitated for a life in the open plains. The 1,214 acres of lively grasslands are viewed by visitors from a 1.5-mile-long bridge, so definitely bring your binoculars or long camera lenses to see it all! The rescued lions, tigers, bears, and wolves go about their natural routines of Eat, Play, Nap while humans can enjoy their company from a distance. There's something so oddly moving about watching a monstrous grizzly bear just poke around her favorite shrub and eventually plop down for a snooze.

The Wild Animal Sanctuary's primary mission is to provide a real life to these neglected animals, and secondary to that is to impart education about these animals onto us. The grounds are open daily (some major holidays excluded) from 9 a.m. to sunset, so it's recommended to visit during active times such as dawn. The sanctuary draws an extremely respectful crowd that is invested in the animals' stories more than in entertainment. The organization also owns a much larger, more remote refuge deeper in the mountains, but in the interest of its inhabitants, they have preserved it away from the public eye. Your heart will be filled with fuzzy feelings when you see the bright orange tigers bathing each other under the shade.

39. WASH PARK: THE LAND OF A THOUSAND NETS

If you wind up in a field with volleyball nets perfectly lined up as far as the eye can see, you've found Wash Park. At the center of a walkable, historic neighborhood is the rectangle-shaped park that spans 10 blocks long and 3 blocks wide. In addition to the thriving pick-up volleyball scene, every activity you can imagine is encouraged here (I once had to swerve past a preteen who was carrying a legitimate sword). Along the perimeter of the park are lanes for bikers and pedestrians, but don't be surprised when you get passed by hoverboards, roller skaters, and off-leash dogs too. This paved walkway makes for a pleasant stroll while you people-watch and ogle at the stunning park-side estates.

At the north tip of Wash Park there's a pond that people can rent watercrafts to tool around on, but keep in mind swimming is not permitted. For an active day, the park has basketball courts that are usually occupied with pickup games, first-come-first-serve tennis courts, and a big playground for children. On weekends, Wash Park is THE volleyball destination. As a lifelong volleyballer myself, I can honestly say I have never seen so many nets in one place. The "official" etiquette is teams of four challenging one another; winner stays on. The park has plenty of space to spread out, so even when it's teeming with volleyball games, you can still find a large patch of grass for a frisbee circle, Spikeball match, or yoga session. Wash Park brings in people from all over the city who want to play outdoors.

40. A PICTURESQUE AFTERNOON AT CHEESEMAN PARK

Deep within a historic neighborhood, is a marble pavilion settled atop a rolling, green field. This urban sanctuary, Cheeseman Park, is comprised of luscious lawns, pathways, playgrounds, and even a small dirt bike park where people of all ages commandeer. The park's pavilion, which resembles the ancient Parthenon in Athens, is used for all purposes such as Quinceañera photo ops or dance practices. In this stone structure, I've even witnessed a proposal; with rose petals sprinkled around a champagne bottle, the couple toasted to themselves as the orange sun dipped beneath the mountains. There's almost always a group meet-up going down at the pavilion, so you never know when you're going to stumble across the roller-skating get-together or a live DJ mixing for a crowd.

The park also hosts the annual Cheeseman Park Art Walk and is the starting point for our annual Denver Pride Parade. In the heart of the park, dogs roam free making friends with nearby folks. The park rangers have been coming out lately to enforce the no off-leash policy, but they know it's loosely followed by parkgoers, so just keep a cautious eye out for anybody in an official-looking uniform before you start your game of fetch. At the park, you might occasionally walk through an odd pocket of cold air. Some say it's just the way the air settles on the grounds, but locals know the truth behind the paranormal sensations. It is a fact that Cheeseman Park originated as a cemetery in the 1800s but was eventually turned into a park by the city. During that time, the deceased were unburied and relocated, but according to public records, it was a botched job that left many bodies still underground. Even with that twisted history, I can feel the positive energy radiating off the park as people mingle alongside our beautiful nature.

41. ALL TYPES OF ACTIVITIES AT RUBY HILL PARK

When the traffic to the mountains is just too unbearable, you can get your skiing or snowboarding fix right here in Denver. At Ruby Hill Park the city sets up a free terrain park for winter where you can hit box features, rails, and jumps without all the ski day hassles. All skill levels and ages are welcome, so don't be intimidated to show up no matter what tricks you can throw. Denver Parks and Rec blows snow to keep the hill safe for use while the gnarly features are thanks to Winter Park Resort — so you know you're in great hands! Yes, you'll have to trek up the Ruby Hill Rail Yard as there are no lifts to transport you once you reach the bottom, but with free rental gear on Thursdays and Saturdays, it's worth the short climbs! If you're wary about catching air, you can partake in a more leisurely winter activity at the designated sledding hill.

In the summertime, the park comes alive with green thumbs tending to plants in the community garden. For thrill-seekers, you can soar through the bike park where ramps will launch you skyward after every tight turn. This park is so massive that it even has three softball fields and an outdoor pool. On summer nights people flock to Ruby Hill Park for its music series at the outdoor Levitt Pavilion, a petite amphitheater with a big mission. The Levitt Pavilion Denver is a part of the larger Levitt Foundation, which is a non-profit that uses its venues to foster unity through free events. At this gathering place, local artists, vendors, and musicians congregate to promote their diverse work while making entertainment more accessible to Denverites.

WAYS TO BE ACTIVE

42. JOIN THE VOLO FAD

There seems to be a refusal amongst Denverites to let go of the competitive sports we played in high school and college. Fortunately, a company capitalized on our love of games by establishing a city-wide intramural league for every organized hobby imaginable. From cup-in-hand kickball to flag football to bar games, there is a Volo Sports league for *everybody*. During summer you'll see Volo games going on at every park across the city, distinguished by players wearing the league's cheap, mismatched t-shirts. You pay for a spot on a team you've established with friends or can go as a solo agent, which is how plenty of newbies make connections! (I've met many soon-to-be-besties under the trying circumstances of a semi-competitive grass volleyball game.)

Your whole league will play on the same night, so you'll be able to check out the competition or just mingle with them! Although Volo is a slightly ill-equipped business (they're known for subpar supplies and uncertain scheduling) it brings coworkers, friends, and strangers together like nothing else. I get a fuzzy feeling when I pass someone wearing a Volo t-shirt, which happens often because I know we are a part of the same active community.

43. GET A GRIP WITH MOVEMENT CLIMBING

When we can't make it to the mountains, we can get out rock-climbing fix at the Movement gyms in the city. These ginormous warehouse spaces offer tons of bouldering (without rope support) and belaying (with the rope system) courses that are regularly rearranged. Although I've been to these gyms plenty of times, I'm still slowly maneuvering up the easiest route while other Denverites are hanging upside down by their fingertips. So, if you're not much of a climber, you could go just to observe the sheer strength of these athletes! These gyms have a vast collection of rock walls for every level and offer challenges for other skills such as traversing sideways or problem-solving.

Rock climbing seems to be the type of sport where you usually walk away better than you started because there's always a new level to master. I love the energy in the gym that fosters comradery as people are giving tips to others or cheering them on during a difficult section. Don't be afraid to ask nearby climbers to give feedback on your technique, the whole point is to learn from each other! The Movement gym in RiNo is connected to an equally giant patio bar, Improper City, where people are always assembling after their arms grow weak. This location is bouldering only, so to test your rope skills you would go to the Movement in Baker for higher thrills. These days every Denverite has a pair of rock-climbing shoes, a chalk bag for better hand grip, and a membership to Movement.

44. GOLF MEETS URBAN LIFE

On a sunny, low-wind day, Denverites head to the golf course, and with an abundance in the metro area, they don't have to go too far. The Denver Golf organization manages eight public courses that are within reach when staying in town. My advice is to get a tee time as early as possible to avoid that midday broil! The City Park Golf Course is located inside City Park, where you can still get views of our skyline behind the historic neighborhood while putting on the green. Fortunately, despite my frequent travels along the road that borders this course, no one has ever whacked a ball into my car!

The other Denver Golf-owned courses are scattered around town offering different scenery and programs for all ages (such as footgolf if you prefer to use your soccer techniques instead of an iron). Since the green is a natural habitat for pollinators, two of Denver Golf's courses oversee thriving honeybee hives, but don't worry they're contained a comfortable distance away from the golfers! There is also golfing in Cherry Creek's Denver Country Club which provides a more formal atmosphere for those who enjoy tradition. If caddying between holes isn't your thing, you can stay in one place at either of the two Topgolf's in Denver. This tech-enhanced multi-floor driving range facilitates all types of target games for patrons while you're served food and beverages in a personal lounge area. There's no better way to hit par with your loved ones than against the backdrop of the front-range mountains.

45. YES, WE'RE OBSESSED WITH PICKLEBALL

Ask any Denverite and they'll say we were an early adopter of the pickleball craze – hey, maybe we even started it! Tennis courts are being cut in half by tiny nets, court reservations are booked days out and the competition is getting fierce. Fortunately, people of all ages have turned to this new hobby, so you'll have no problem finding a partner or group that matches whatever your level of seriousness is. You can hear the donks and dinks from anywhere in town, so most courts close up after dark to maintain the restful shuteye we all deserve. Every rec center now accommodates pickleball one way or another, such as the Gates Tennis Center, which now splits its loyalty to tennis and pickleballers alike. Camp Pickle will soon be the hottest drink and play destination in town with construction commencing on multiple industrial-sized complexes. Once the sport of pickleball came to Denver it spread like our late-summer wildfires.

46. MAKE TIME TO SWEAT

On those brutally warm afternoons or frigid winter evenings when you still need to get a workout in, Denver has an array of indoor options. As you may guess, the city is bountiful with yoga studios that offer anything from puff'n'pose classes to power yoga. YogaBox has opened several studios in the Denver metro where you'll do challenging movements in a heated room under aesthetic neon lighting. On the other end of the spectrum is Urban Sanctuary, a minority women-owned space focusing on channeling divine spirituality through movement. Apex Denver, one of my favorite concepts, is an acrobatics-slash-parkour gym where you can experiment on their trampolines during open gym times or take circus-inspired classes by seasoned vets. Under their instruction, I've been able to perfect my backflip and learn how to scale up a wall!

The biggest traditional gym in the city is the Denver Athletic Club which provides avenues for every type of fitness activity possible. It's a bougie facility with everything from squash courts to an indoor pool, so you could spend a whole day there. The Carla Madison Rec Center has a less upscale attitude if you need to pump some iron or shoot free throws without all the extra amenities. Our various dance studios will reignite your passion for hip-hop, Zumba, and even pole dancing! Denverites seem to love their fitness classes which is why F45, Orangetheory, Pure Barre, 9Round Kickboxing, and many other niche studios have popped up on every corner.

SHOPPING

47. THE REI FLAGSHIP

Shopping at our flagship REI (standing for Recreational Equipment, Inc.) is a popular pastime of us Denverites. This giant brick building towering over the Platte River consists of three stories, a rock wall, a Starbucks, and any sporting good you can think of! "Gearheads" (those who splurge on state-of-the-art equipment) can spend hours navigating through the endless isles of every item related to camping, skiing, biking, river rafting, and so on. The REI can be a fun window-shopping adventure too, I find enjoyment in just browsing all the innovative gadgets I didn't even know existed!

Our REI also has a robust membership program that lets us in on their frequent deals and offers us an exclusive Trade-In / Used Gear inventory on its top floor. This one-stop shop is truly our lifeline for outdoor recreation because they even facilitate bike repairs, ski tune-ups, and rentals for all types of gear. REI engages the community by also hosting tons of educational workshops and guided trips. Before embarking on an expedition through the Rocky Mountains, you can take an REI class on Wilderness

First Aid, Compass Navigation, or even Outdoor Photography! I've known many friends to take their rock-climbing courses and then go on to be avid (and safe) climbers capable of doing some pretty difficult routes. REI makes the outdoors accessible to all of us in Denver; therefore, I would highly encourage you to visit this flagship location or do an experience with them to see how important it is to our community.

48. THRIFT 'TIL YOU DROP

As a devoted thrifter, I can say Denver's thrift scene does not disappoint. With residents who love recycled items and take pride in their style, there is no shortage of secondhand clothes circulating throughout the city. If you don't want to narrow your search down to one store you could start with attending Thrift-Pop, a monthly outdoor thrift event hosted on the last Sunday of every month (this can be dependent on our weather, so make sure to visit their website before you go).

The main thrift store you may hear of is our Arcs, which are located at every corner of the city. Arc is a perfect thrift store for treasure hunters who love to take their time sifting through racks and racks of eccentric clothes to find that one take-home item. It can be a bit daunting to take on the massive inventory, so friends of mine advise making a whole afternoon out of it. The Arc stores, as well as Atomic Salvage and Boss all lean on the vintage, funky side if that's your jam! If you're looking for an unusual pre-game spot, Garage Sale is a lively bar-slash-vintage shop that will serve you a marg while you shop for that bomber jacket you've always dreamed of.

I must mention Déjà Blue, a Goodwill Boutique Store that sells interesting high-end garments, although I've never personally lucked out at this one. Speaking of Goodwill, their vast location on South Broadway has been said by several of my friends to be the "best Goodwill I've ever seen". With preserved glassware and tons of in-style items, I drop in here when I'm really on a budget.

Lastly, we used to have a Buffalo Exchange, but rumor has it a vindictive ownership scandal caused the popular store to close its doors. On a happier note, in its exact place now stands my personal favorite thrift store: Crossroads, a modern thrift store with trendy, quality brands. I always walk away with a pre-loved outfit that somehow looks better than if I had bought the clothes new!

49. WHERE THE BOOKWORMS GO

On a snowy or rainy day, I cozy up in my favorite bookstore of all time: Tattered Cover on Colfax. This Colorado-only franchise has locations throughout the state and multiple in the Denver metro, but the one on Colfax gives me whimsical-library-at-a-magic-boarding-school vibes. The store has a small coffee shop at the entrance, which will perk you up for the adventure that awaits. On the main level, a labyrinth of wooden bookshelves standing 30 feet tall carries everything from bestsellers to fantasy to even poems. I love the idea that when you walk into this bookstore the possibilities are truly endless. I've left this bookstore with crossword puzzles, cookbooks, journals, and countless new stories to devour.

If you find your way to the hidden basement, you'll be met with their used book and local author section (the secret is to turn left when you walk in, then descend the cavern-like tunnel). I love that the staff has planted hand-written reviews all throughout each section with their testimonials of the books they've read, although it can sometimes make my decision next to impossible! Tattered Cover has a packed calendar of events where they host topical discussions or readings from authors on a weekly basis. They also run book clubs for all ages and genres, so no reader is left behind. Come voyage through brand new worlds in the archives of this charmed book-lover sanctuary.

TAKE MEMORIES, LEAVE BEAUTY
50. AN ECO-CONSCIOUS VISIT

As an environmentalist myself, I know our outdoorsy haven has been made possible by the eco-consciousness of our residents and visitors. There is great responsibility in protecting our beautiful city so that we can enjoy the lifestyle so closely intertwined with our nature. My last piece of wisdom to bestow on you is how to execute this eco-conscious mindset during your travels.

Denverites operate under a Leave No Trace policy, meaning whether we're camping or just having a picnic at the park, we ensure everything we brought with us goes back in our bags as we depart. It's no secret that artificial materials are harmful to nature, but even leaving biodegradable fruit peels or dog waste can disrupt an ecosystem that it is foreign to, so the practice really is to leave *no* trace. A tiny but mighty act that my friend group participates in is picking up the occasional litter we spot around town. On a heartwarming note, I've witnessed passersby noticing our humble efforts and begin cleaning up as well.

I'm a big believer in 'bring-your-owns', so I suggest tooling around town with a reusable tote bag, a steel water bottle, and even a glass Tupperware to store any leftovers in! If you forgot the shampoo at home or need literally any other household supply, you can hit our Off the Bottle Refill Shop where they even have free glass jars for those who don't have an empty container to spare. We have recently rolled out a citywide compost program that should be required for most businesses, so ask the place you're staying if they have a compost bin for your breakfast burrito scraps when you just can't shove down any more of its deliciousness. To lead a low-emissions visit, I suggest walking or scootering around town — plus that's the best way to truly immerse yourself in any new place! My rule of thumb is to always think of the Earth's integrity before addressing my own needs. Visiting Denver will remind you just how special our relationship with nature can be.

Travel Like a Local

So, the rumors you've heard are true: sitting at 5,267 feet above sea level Denver is, in fact, our nation's Mile High City. With a remarkable climate system, juxtaposed traits, and a blossoming culture Denver is a one-of-a-kind destination to explore. Our city, known for its copious "we're *elevated*" and "let's get *high*" puns, is a special outdoor oasis amidst a thriving urban collective. By traveling like a local you will experience natural beauty and the social scene that my fascinating home has in store for you.

TOP THREE REASONS TO BOOK THIS TRIP

The Endless Outdoors. Every escapade around Denver will remind you of the incredible nature we're surrounded by. Our city is home to infinite gardens, parks, and pathways that will connect you to the outdoors while the Rocky Mountains sit right within reach.

The Creative Scene. Denver will inspire your imagination through its emphasis on art and music. You can fuel your curiosity with the abundance of art walks, festivals, installations, and concerts. Our city encourages originality in all forms of discussion, movement, fashion, and creation.

The Active Lifestyle. You can never get bored when visiting Denver — but you will sleep well at night — because all year round the city is buzzing with activities. In summer, you'll play pick-up volleyball at the park or bike along the Platte River. In winter, you'll sled down Ruby Hill Park or boulder at the indoor rock-climbing gym. You'll be your healthiest, most energetic self when it's all said and done.

RESOURCES FOR FURTHER EXPLORATION

Official Government Website - https://www.denvergov.org/

Official Visitation Website - https://www.denver.org/

Indie News Website (Entertainment and Pop Culture) - https://www.westword.com/

News Website (Culture and Politics) - https://denverite.com/

News Website (Breaking News) - https://www.denverpost.com/

APPS & SOCIALS

Instagram

Entertainment, Pop Culture, and Food - @denverwestword

Entertainment, Pop Culture, and Food - @do303official

Events – @5280 magazine

Events - @visitDenver

Public Parking - ParkMobile

Public Transit - RTD MyRide

Food and Beverage – Eat+Drink Denver Pass

Walking and Hiking Paths Nearby – AllTrails

DID YOU KNOW?

We sit on a flat plain 12 miles from the start of our famous mountain range, meaning Denver is actually in the high desert! With our year-round clear blue skies, Denver averages nearly 300 days of sunshine. Even the so-called sunny state of Florida is outshined by our climate.

Cooking requires a different attitude at our mile-high altitude! At this elevation, water boils at a lower temperature; therefore, even if it seems like your pasta has been rumbling for a while, just be patient because it's technically being cooked at a lower temperature.

The Denver metro as we know it is the result of the mid-1800s gold rush. Once a smidgen of gold was uncovered in our South Platte and Cherry Creek rivers, the area was immediately thrown together as an official city. Long before the gold rush seams burst open, Indigenous tribes congregated on the land.

TRAVEL BUCKET LIST

1.

2.

3.

4.

5.

6.

7.

8.

9.

10.

TRIVIA

1. What location in Denver is exactly one mile (5,280 feet) high in elevation?

2. How many Michelin stars have been awarded in Denver?

3. What is the name of the longest continuous street in the U.S. that runs right through Denver?

4. What year did Denver host the Olympics?

5. What famous actor of the Santa Clause movies was born in Denver?

6. What contemporary indie-folk band of the songs "Ho Hey" and "Ophelia" originated in Denver?

7. How many professional sports teams does Denver have?

8. What folk-rock legend changed his surname to honor his beloved (but not hometown) city?

9. What Denver native and mischievous businesswoman invented a revolutionary children's toy?

10. What is the oldest restaurant in Denver?

1. The 13th Step of our Capitol building's west-facing side is exactly one mile high (for now). Due to precision advancements in technology, the mile marker has already been moved around several times.

2. None! Not to worry though, lots of impeccable restaurants are racing to be the first.

3. Colfax Avenue, which stretches over 50 miles long.

4. Trick question! Denver remains the only city to have denied their winning Olympic bid. We'll never know what could have been in 1976.

5. Tim Allen was born here in 1953 before he made his name as the jolly red fellow.

6. The Lumineers first created their moody ballads in Denver.

7. We have a whopping 6 pro teams (Football, Hockey, Soccer, Basketball, Baseball, and even Lacrosse).

8. John Denver treasured our city so much that he just had to have its name!

9. Denverite Ruth Handler invented the iconic Barbie doll, named after her daughter Barbara.

10. Operating since 1893, The Buckhorn Exchange still dishes out steakhouse classics.

PACKING AND PLANNING TIPS

A Week before Leaving

- Arrange for someone to take care of pets and water plants.

- Email and Print important Documents.

- Get Visa and vaccines if needed.

- Check for travel warnings.

- Stop mail and newspaper.

- Notify Credit Card companies where you are going.

- Passports and photo identification is up to date.

- Pay bills.

- Copy important items and download travel Apps.

- Start collecting small bills for tips.

- Have post office hold mail while you are away.

- Check weather for the week.

- Car inspected, oil is changed, and tires have the correct pressure.

- Check airline luggage restrictions.

- Download Apps needed for your trip.

Right Before Leaving

- Contact bank and credit cards to tell them your location.

- Clean out refrigerator.

- Empty garbage cans.

- Lock windows.

- Make sure you have the proper identification with you.

- Bring cash for tips.

- Remember travel documents.

- Lock door behind you.

- Remember wallet.

- Unplug items in house and pack chargers.

- Change your thermostat settings.

- Charge electronics, and prepare camera memory cards.

READ OTHER TRAVEL BOOKS FROM CZYK PUBLISHING

Greater Than a Tourist- California: 50 Travel Tips from Locals

Greater Than a Tourist- Salem Massachusetts USA 50 Travel Tips from a Local by Danielle Lasher

Greater Than a Tourist United States: 50 Travel Tips from Locals

Greater Than a Tourist- St. Croix US Virgin Islands USA: 50 Travel Tips from a Local by Tracy Birdsall

Greater Than a Tourist- Montana: 50 Travel Tips from a Local by Laurie White

Children's Book: Charlie the Cavalier Travels the World by Lisa Rusczyk Ed. D.

CZYKPublishing.com

METRIC CONVERSIONS

TEMPERATURE

110° F —
100° F —
90° F — — 40° C
80° F —
70° F — — 30° C
60° F —
50° F — — 20° C
40° F — — 10° C
32° F — — 0° C
20° F —
10° F — — -10° C
0° F — — -18° C
-10° F —
-20° F — — -30° C

To convert F to C:

Subtract 32, and then multiply by 5/9 or .5555.

To Convert C to F:

Multiply by 1.8
and then add 32.

32F = 0C

LIQUID VOLUME

To Convert:...................Multiply by
U.S. Gallons to Liters................. 3.8
U.S. Liters to Gallons 26
Imperial Gallons to U.S. Gallons 1.2
Imperial Gallons to Liters....... 4.55
Liters to Imperial Gallons 22
1 Liter = .26 U.S. Gallon
1 U.S. Gallon = 3.8 Liters

DISTANCE

To convert ....Multiply by
Inches to Centimeters 2.54
Centimeters to Inches 39
Feet to Meters........................ .3
Meters to Feet 3.28
Yards to Meters 91
Meters to Yards 1.09
Miles to Kilometers 1.61
Kilometers to Miles............ .62
1 Mile = 1.6 km
1 km = .62 Miles

WEIGHT

1 Ounce = .28 Grams
1 Pound = .4555 Kilograms
1 Gram = .04 Ounce
1 Kilogram = 2.2 Pounds

TRAVEL QUESTIONS

- Do you bring presents home to family or friends after a vacation?

- Do you get motion sick?

- Do you have a favorite billboard?

- Do you know what to do if there is a flat tire?

- Do you like a sun roof open?

- Do you like to eat in the car?

- Do you like to wear sun glasses in the car?

- Do you like toppings on your ice cream?

- Do you use public bathrooms?

- Did you bring a cell phone and does it have power?

- Do you have a form of identification with you?

- Have you ever been pulled over by a cop?

- Have you ever given money to a stranger on a road trip?

- Have you ever taken a road trip with animals?

- Have you ever gone on a vacation alone?

- Have you ever run out of gas?

- If you could move to any place in the world, where would it be?

- If you could travel anywhere in the world, where would you travel?

- If you could travel in any vehicle, which one would it be?

- If you had three things to wish for from a magic genie, what would they be?

- If you have a driver's license, how many times did it take you to pass the test?

- What are you the most afraid of on vacation?

- What do you want to get away from the most when you are on vacation?

- What foods smell bad to you?

- What item do you bring on ever trip with you away from home?

- What makes you sleepy?

- What song would you love to hear on the radio when you're cruising on the highway?

- What travel job would you want the least?

- What will you miss most while you are away from home?

- What is something you always wanted to try?

- What is the best road side attraction that you ever saw?

- What is the farthest distance you ever biked?

Made in United States
Troutdale, OR
12/19/2024

26923836R00070